P9-CLO-192

Stefen Bernath

THE CACTUS
Coloring Book

With an introduction & captions by
Carolyn S. Ripps

Former Director, The New York Cactus
and Succulent Society

Dover Publications, Inc.
New York

INTRODUCTION

Cacti are among the most remarkable and most misunderstood plants in the world. Although some species are capable of surviving in deserts, others flourish in habitats ranging from tropical jungles to windswept mountainsides.

All cacti are members of the one plant family *Cactaceae*. Whatever their natural habitat, they all share a few botanical features, among which is the presence of unique structures called areoles. These are fuzzy spots on the surface of the plant from which the spines, hairs, leaves, and sometimes the flowers arise. If a succulent (water-storing) plant does not have areoles, it's not a cactus! Those succulents which are not cacti may be found in many other plant families. Cacti are native to the Americas, but cactus plants and seeds have been spread around the world since ancient times, and cacti may today be found growing almost anywhere.

Like all plants, cacti need light and water, especially during periods of active growth. The ability of some species to survive in desert environments comes from their capacity to absorb and conserve whatever moisture is available from rain, fog or dew. Many succulent plants, including cacti, have reduced or lost their leaves. The plants consist of waxy globular or columnar stems which minimize surface area and water loss. Many have developed dense coverings of hair or spines to shade the plant bodies from intense sunlight.

Flowering often coincides with the beginning of the rainy season, enabling the plants to complete their reproductive cycle under the most favorable conditions.

Cactus flowers are some of the most beautiful in the world, but few people have been fortunate enough to see many cacti in bloom. While some of the species illustrated in this book are not suitable for home cultivation, many of the small ones are excellent house plants and can be flowered on a sunny windowsill with a minimum of care. Many of our native cacti can withstand the rigors of frost and snow. The winter-hardy varieties, some of which are mentioned in the captions, would make unusual additions to an outdoor perennial garden.

In order to achieve normal growth and flowering as house plants, cacti must receive balanced amounts of sunlight and water. While it is difficult to give cultural instructions which apply to all cacti, most of the non-epiphytic, that is, terrestrial, species will respond satisfactorily with the following care.

During the fall and winter months, when there is little sunshine, most cacti go dormant. During this essential resting period, the plants must be kept relatively dry and at 45° F., if possible. Light is far less important at this time of the year. While dormant, cacti should be watered only enough to keep them from shrivelling, perhaps once a month.

In spring, or whenever the plants show signs of resuming growth, watering should be increased gradually. In the hottest days of summer, plants growing in full sunshine may need to be watered thoroughly every 2 to 3 days. Dilute solutions of balanced plant food high in phosphorus should be given in the spring and summer to promote flowering.

Any porous, rapidly draining potting soil of approximately neutral acidity will be satisfactory for most cacti. A typical soil mix might contain 2 parts of humusy soil, 1 part of peat moss, and 1 part of builders' sand or bird gravel. Small amounts of lime may

(continued on p. 46)

Copyright

Copyright © 1981 by Dover Publications, Inc.
All rights reserved.

Bibliographical Note

The Cactus Coloring Book is a new work, first published by Dover Publications, Inc., in 1981.

International Standard Book Number

ISBN-13: 978-0-486-24097-8
ISBN-10: 0-486-24097-5

Manufactured in the United States by LSC Communications
24097525   2019
www.doverpublications.com

OPUNTIA BASILARIS (*Beaver tail cactus*). Arizona, Nevada, California, Mexico. When people think of desert cacti, these flat-jointed plants usually come to mind. There are more species of Opuntia than any other cactus, and they are distributed throughout the Americas. Some are winter-hardy, provided they are situated in a sunny location with well-drained soil. As house plants, they require full sun, little water and a completely dry, cool winter rest or they will assume an unnaturally elongated shape. Opuntias often bear glochids, barbed bristles which are readily detached and embedded in skin or clothes. This specimen is a lovely blue-green, compensating for the fact that it seldom flowers indoors.

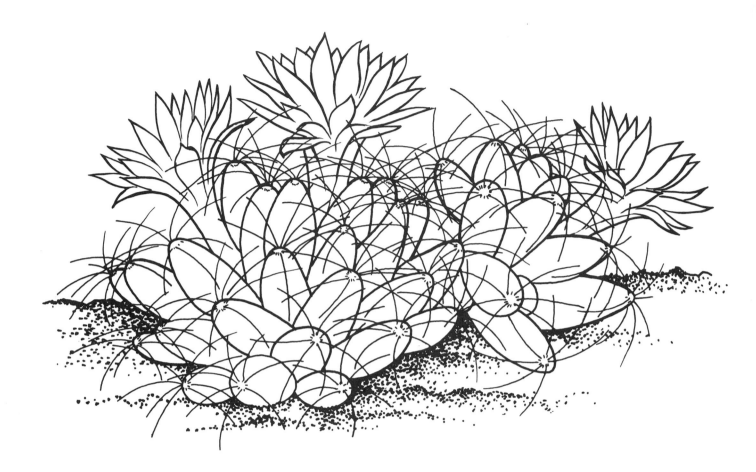

Above: **DOLICOTHELE LONGIMAMMA** (*Nipple cactus*). Mexico. A compact, clustering cactus with very long, thin tubercles, or bumps, bearing curved spines. It is a good species for indoor growing, requiring rich, porous soil and average water. Keep at about 50° F. in winter and withhold water. Plants may be propagated by rooting offsets or individual tubercles. The large, yellow flowers are produced freely in full sun.

Opposite: **OPUNTIA BIGELOVII** (*Teddy bear cholla*). Arizona, Nevada, California, northern Mexico. This densely spined desert plant may grow to a height of six feet. The segmented joints are easily detached from the parent plant, giving it another common name, "jumping cholla." These spiny sections are often used by desert mammals to provide a protective barrier at the entrance to their burrows. It has purple flowers in spring, followed by large, yellow fruits.

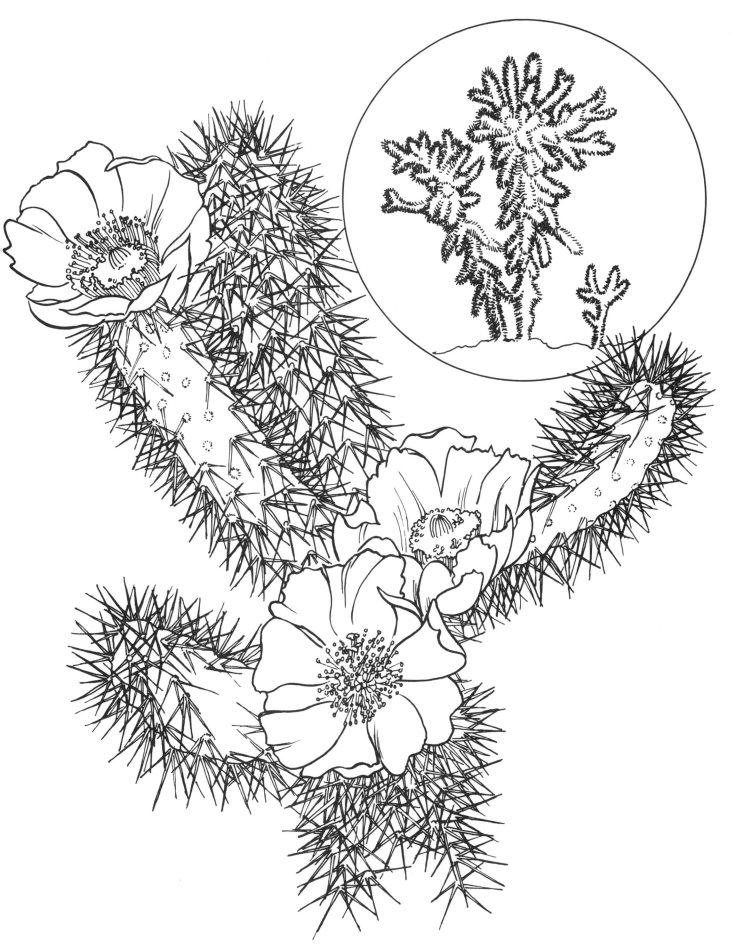

Above: **LOPHOPHORA WILLIAMSII** (*Peyote*). Texas and Mexico. A slow-growing, spineless, blue-green cactus having tufts of white wool at the areoles. It has long, tuberous roots and requires a deep container with a porous soil mix. Water sparingly in summer and not at all in winter. Dried sliced *Lophophora* plants, referred to as "mescal buttons," are sometimes ingested by native tribes of the southwestern U.S. and northern Mexico in order to induce hallucinogenic effects from mescaline and other alkaloids which they contain. Pink flowers are readily produced in summer, followed by red fruits.

Opposite: **CEPHALOCEREUS SENILIS** (*Old man cactus*). Mexico. A most attractive house plant with its dense covering of white hairs. It requires full sun, a porous soil with added limestone, and less than average water at all times. In nature, plants may grow to a height of fifty feet, bearing rose-colored flowers on a lateral cephalium, that part of the stem with the thickest growth of hair. Indoors, this species usually will not flower.

ENCEPHALOCARPUS STROBILIFORMIS (*Pinecone cactus*). Mexico. Small, very slow-growing and rare, it requires full sun and very porous soil. Provide water very sparingly at all times. Must be kept completely dry and slightly warm in winter. Areoles and spines are found only on the youngest part of the plant and are soon lost. The red-violet flowers are relatively large. Only one species of Encephalocarpus is known to exist.

6

ASTROPHYTUM ASTERIAS (*Sand dollar*). Texas and Mexico. A small, spineless cactus which can be grown as a house plant in very porous soil with careful watering. Even when not in flower, it is extremely attractive with its pattern of white spots and gray tufts of wool at the areoles. In its normal habitat, this species is found partially shaded by bushes and tall grass, so it does not require intense sun to maintain its normal shape. The large yellow flowers have vivid red centers.

TOUMEYA PAPYRACANTHA (*Gramma grass cactus*).
Arizona and New Mexico. The spines of this curious cactus
are thin and papery, like the mountain grasses among which
it grows. Provide a rich, sandy soil with added leaf mold;
water sparingly. Keep cold and completely dry in winter.
The green and white flowers usually do not open fully.

ECHINOFOSSULOCACTUS MULTICOSTATUS or STENOCACTUS MULTICOSTATUS (*Brain cactus*). Mexico. This species is native to high, grassy meadowlands and requires rich, porous soil, average summer watering, and good sun. Although not free-flowering indoors, it remains attractive year-round because of its numerous surface ribs. Keep cool and dry during winter. In spring, white flowers with purple centers are borne at the top of the plant.

GYMNOCALYCIUM MIHANOVICHII (*Plaid chin cactus*) **and GYMNOCALYCIUM MIHANOVICHII V. FRIED-RICHIAE "HIBOTAN"** (*Red cap*). Paraguay. Probably the easiest cactus to grow and flower as a house plant. In a half-sunny location, it will bloom all summer, and should be watered generously. In winter, keep slightly warm and water occasionally to keep plants from shrivelling. Flowers are combinations of white, pink and green. The color of the plant bodies also varies considerably. Highly colored yellow, orange or pink plants, deficient in chlorophyll, must be grown as grafts on other types of cacti. These grafted plants seldom flower and must be kept warmer and given more water in winter than the plant grown on its own roots.

PELECYPHORA ASELLIFORMIS. Mexico. An unusual dwarf species which requires full sun and a porous soil rich in organic material. Keep cool and completely dry in winter. The flat gray-brown tubercles are compressed and "hatchet-shaped." The grooved areoles bear two rows of flattened spines resembling a double-edged comb. Pink flowers, which may be an inch in diameter, arise from the top of the plant. The native Mexicans use this plant in the same way as *L. williamsii*, and often refer to it by the same common name.

11

MAMMILLARIA WILDII. Mexico. An easily grown house plant which requires only moderate sunshine in summer and average soil, watering, and cultural conditions, including a cool, dry winter rest. It produces many red-striped flowers all summer. The attractive red seed pods from the previous year's flowers persist for long periods of time.

GYMNOCALYCIUM VENTURIANUM or GYMNO-CALYCIUM BALDIANUM (*Rainbow chin cactus*). Argentina and Uruguay. An excellent house plant. Provide a rich soil and ample summer water. During the winter, keep above 50° F. and water about once a month. All Gymnocalyciums are highly recommended for indoor growing. They will flower throughout the summer in a half-sunny location. The deep-red flower color is unusual in this genus.

MAMMILLARIA HAHNIANA (*Old lady cactus*). Mexico. When grown in full sunlight, this species will be covered with long, silky white hairs. It needs a well-drained soil with added limestone and less than average water. Keep dry and provide a little winter warmth. Most Mammillarias are excellent house plants, having abundant or colorful flowers on compact plants with interesting spine patterns. Small magenta flowers are produced in a ring around the top of the plant in summer.

EPITHELANTHA MICROMERIS (*Button cactus*). Texas, New Mexico and Mexico. These cacti are noteworthy for the complex, lacy network of white spines which cover the plant body. They do not require constant intense sun, but should be given less water than average and none in winter. A porous, sandy soil with extra limestone added is essential. Small pink flowers in spring are followed by tubular red fruit.

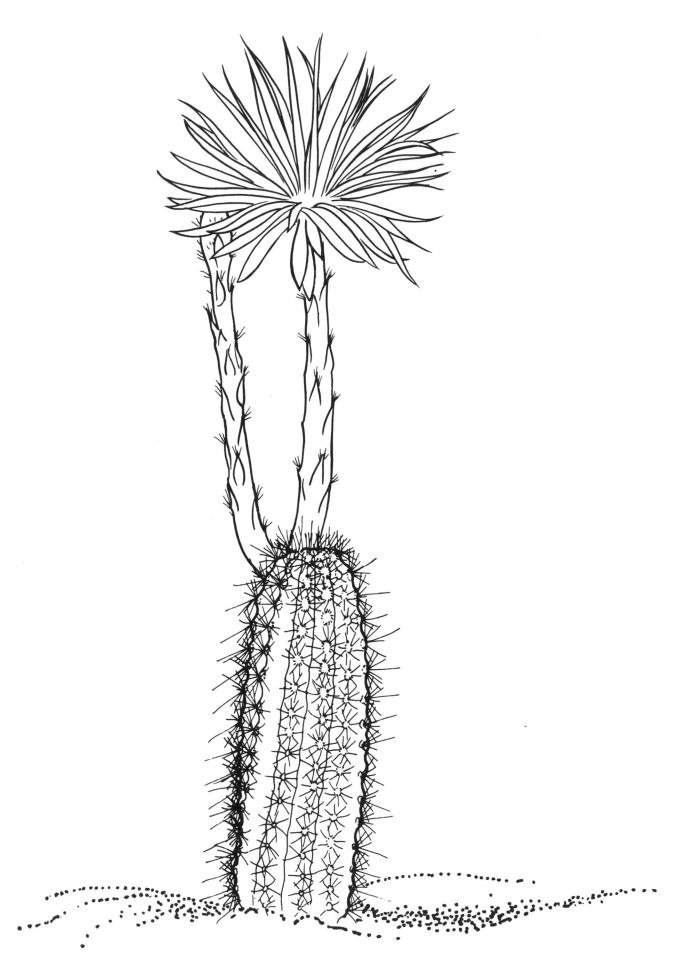

Opposite: **SETIECHINOPSIS MIRABILIS** (*Flower of prayer*). Argentina. A small, dark brown columnar plant which seldom grows taller than six inches. The plants are easily grown from seed and may begin to flower in their second year (average cactus soil and cultural conditions). This is the only species of Setiechinopsis known. It produces long, fragrant white flowers which open at sunset and last only a few hours.

Above: **CORYPHANTHA VIVIPARA** (*Beehive cactus*). Arizona and Nevada north into Canada. A small-growing species which is widely distributed throughout the central United States. The northern forms of this plant are winter-hardy, even into Canada. As a house plant, it requires good light and regular watering during the summer with a dry, cold winter rest period. It bears fringed, fragrant pink flowers in midsummer.

ARIOCARPUS FISSURATUS (*Living rock cactus*). Mexico. A very slow-growing species which appers lifeless due to its rock-hard texture and dark, fissured skin. Only the appearance of the purplish-pink flowers or a slight increase in the amount of wool at the top of the plant identifies periods of "active" growth. Requires very porous soil with additional lime and a location in full sun. It must be watered very sparingly, even in summer. A long, completely dry winter rest period is essential.

18

NEOBESSEYA MISSOURIENSIS (*Nipple cactus*). Central United States from Louisiana to Colorado. A small plant which is widely distributed in the grassy woodlands of the central United States, it can be grown as a pot plant with average summer care if kept very dry and cold all winter.

This species is completely winter-hardy and may be easily grown outdoors in a sunny, well-drained location. The large red fruits will last for many months and contrast beautifully with the fringed green-brown flowers.

Opposite: **PERESKIA ACULEATA.** West Indies. Thought to be among the most primitive of cacti, Pereskia species bear leaves and may grow into large shrubs. Indoors, they require a soil rich in peat, and more water than the average leafless cactus. Winter temperatures should not be allowed to drop below 50° F., with occasional watering to prevent leaf drop. The stems of Pereskia are often used as grafting stock for other cacti, especially epiphytic types. *Pereskia aculeata var. godseffiana* is a compact form which has red and gold leaves and makes an attractive foliage plant.

Above: **MAMMILLARIA PLUMOSA** (*Feather cactus*). Mexico. A beautiful, small, freely clustering species with white feather-like spines which cover the plant. Requires full sun and less than average water. Keep dry and provide some warmth in winter. Unlike most other Mammillarias, this plant seldom flowers when grown indoors.

Opposite: **CARNEGIEA GIGANTEA** (*Saguaro or sahuaro*). Arizona, California, Mexico. This majestic cactus of the southwestern deserts may reach a height of fifty feet. Birds often nest within cavities in the plant's massive trunk and branches. The five-inch-wide flowers open at night and last only one day. Arizona has chosen *Carnegiea gigantea* as its state flower.

Above: **NOTOCACTUS RUTILANS** (*Pink ball cactus*). Uruguay. Another easily grown species which is a good house plant. Notocacti prefer moderate sun, abundant summer water, and a sandy, humus-rich soil. They must be kept cold and dry in winter. The large pink flowers have an unusual satiny sheen. Most other Notocacti are also recommended for indoor growing.

AZTEKIUM RITTERI. Mexico. A very rare, small species which is in danger of becoming extinct in the wild. It is a difficult house plant, requiring full sun, porous soil with added lime, and less water than average. Keep cool and very dry in winter. The plant body is unique with its folded grayish-green surface. The white flowers are large for the size of the plant.

ASTROPHYTUM CAPRICORNE (*Goat's horn cactus*). Mexico. A satisfactory house plant requiring full sun, additional lime in the soil, and less than average watering. Keep dry in winter and at about 40° F. The large, satiny yellow and red flowers may attain a diameter of three inches. A spineless relative, *A. myriostigma*, is another good plant for indoor growing.

Opposite: **AUSTROCYLINDROPUNTIA SALMIANA or OPUNTIA SALMIANA.** Brazil, Paraguay, Bolivia, Argentina. A shrubby dwarf Opuntia which can be grown as a house plant in a sunny location. Provide rich, well-drained soil and ample water in summer. Keep cool in winter with occasional water to keep plant from shrivelling. This species is not often self-fertile and must be propagated from cuttings. The large yellow flowers contrast beautifully with the red-purple of the young stems.

Above: **ECHINOCEREUS PENTALOPHUS** (*Lady finger cactus*). Texas and Mexico. This sprawling Echinocereus requires full sun and a rich, well-drained soil with a little added lime. Give just enough water in winter to prevent shrivelling and keep above freezing. Outdoors, the stems may reach a length of six inches. Its large, vivid purple flowers are striking.

Opposite: **SELENICEREUS GRANDIFLORUS** (*Queen of the night*). West Indies. A climbing tropical plant widely distributed throughout the Caribbean region. Too large for indoor use except in a greenhouse where it requires abundant water and year-round warmth. It is most notable for its huge white vanilla-scented flowers which open at night and die in less than a day. Aerial roots are numerous along the stems and enable the plant to spread across walls and buildings.

Above: **ECHINOCEREUS TRIGLOCHIDIATUS** (*Claret cup cactus*). An easily grown, small Echinocereus which requires a bit more than average water in summer. It is winter-hardy, if kept very dry. The bright green stigma is characteristic of the genus. The common name is derived from the ruby-red cup-shaped flowers. *E. viridiflorus* is another good indoor plant which is also winter-hardy.

LEUCHTENBERGIA PRINCIPIS (*Agave cactus*). Mexico. A slow-growing atypical cactus with greatly elongated gray-green tubercles and papery spines. This species has a long tap root which requires a deep container and well-drained soil. Provide less than average water in summer. Keep dry and cold in winter. It produces fragrant yellow flowers in full sunshine.

30

ECHINOCACTUS GRUSONII (*Golden barrel cactus*). Mexico. A slow-growing globular plant which may reach a diameter of two feet at maturity. Young plants appear to have prominent tubercles which fuse as the plant matures, forming ribs covered with golden spines. Young specimens may be grown indoors in bright sun with average soil and watering. A cool, dry winter rest period is essential. Only mature plants bear the yellow flowers.

PARODIA SANGUINIFLORA. Argentina. Another good species for a partly sunny indoor location, bearing large "blood-red" flowers in summer. Provide a rich, porous soil and average watering. In winter, keep above 50° F. and water monthly. All Parodias are attractive house plants with their yellow, orange or red flowers and interesting spine patterns.

FRAILEA PYGMAEA. Uruguay and Argentina. An easily grown dwarf species scarcely more than an inch in diameter. All Frailea species require partial shade and a rich soil. Water generously in summer. Unless the weather is very hot, flowers may set seed without ever opening. When the yellow flowers do open, they are almost as large as the plant bodies.

LOBIVIA FAMATIMENSIS. Bolivia and Argentina. A compact plant suitable for indoor culture. It requires a rich soil and average summer watering, but prefers partial summer sun. In winter it may be kept quite cold if water is withheld. A number of varieties are known, having flowers which are orange, red, yellow or pink. Many other Lobivias are good house plants also.

PEDIOCACTUS KNOWLTONII. Colorado and New Mexico. This plant, possibly a variety of *Pediocactus bradyi,* is one of the world's smallest cacti. Mature specimens may not exceed one inch in diameter. It requires a porous soil and less than average water at all times. In its natural habitat, it can withstand some frost. As a pot plant, it should be kept dry and cold in winter. White-pink flowers emerge in early spring.

Above: **HOMALOCEPHALA TEXENSIS** (*Horse crippler*). Texas and New Mexico. A heavily spined plant which may attain a diameter greater than one foot. Requires intense sun, high temperatures and a rich soil for flowering. Keep dry in winter. It bears fragrant, feathery orange and pink flowers followed by large red fruit.

Opposite: **MELOCACTUS INTORTUS** (*Turk's cap cactus*). West Indies. Melocacti prefer sandy humus with ample summer water and partial shade during hot sunny days. They should be kept dry in winter and not allowed to fall below 50° F. Plants do not flower until they are mature enough to produce a cephalium atop the plant body; this may take many years. The small magenta flowers and fruit are borne on the cephalium, a structure which can ultimately reach a height of three feet. Once the cephalium has developed, transplanting is not advisable. Propagate from seed, since plants do not form offsets.

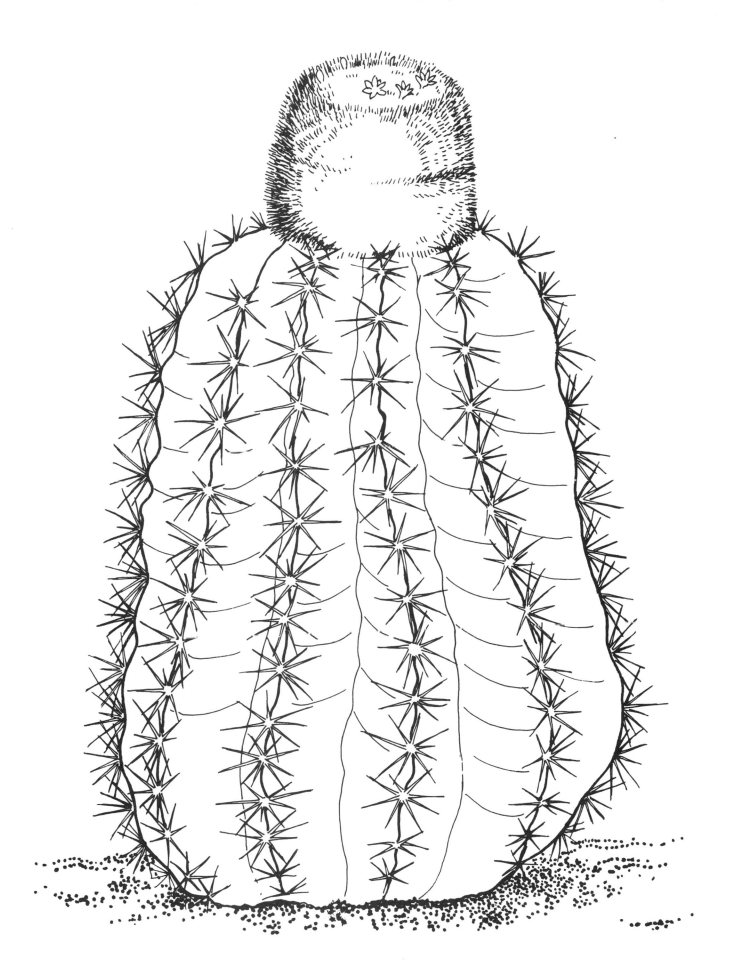

Above: **REBUTIA DEMINUTA or AYLOSTERA DEMI-NUTA.** (*Crown cactus*). Argentina. Cacti of the genus Rebutia are all exceptionally good house plants because of their small size and abundant, colorful flowers. They require a sunny location with ample water once flower buds have appeared. In winter, they must be kept cold (45° F.) and quite dry, or flowering will not occur. This species is one of the most floriferous; a one-inch plant is capable of producing over two dozen flowers in spring. Different species have flowers of pink, yellow, purple, red or orange.

Opposite: **APOROCACTUS FLAGELLIFORMIS** (*Rat's tail cactus*). Mexico. An attractive species which is nicer than its common name would suggest. Give full sun in summer, rich soil and abundant water. This species likes a cool winter rest in good light with occasional watering. It is often grafted onto another cactus to reduce the chances of rotting. A good choice for a hanging basket, it produces abundant pink flowers even when young.

Above: **NOTOCACTUS HASELBERGII** (*Scarlet ball*). Brazil. A compact, white-spined species requiring a sunny location and average soil with moderate watering in summer. This plant needs a long, dry winter rest to ensure flowering, but provide slight warmth. All species of Notocactus are good house plants, flowering readily without elaborate care. The vivid red-orange flowers of this species appear in midsummer.

Opposite: **ZYGOCACTUS TRUNCATUS** (*Christmas cactus*) and **SCHLUMBERGERA GAERTNERI** (*Easter cactus*). Brazil. These epiphytic cacti and their hybrids have been popular house plants for years because of their abundant, colorful flowers. Both require ample summer water and partial shade. Flowering is triggered by short days and cool temperatures. Once flower buds have formed, do not move the plants, as slight changes in environment may cause the buds to drop. There has been extensive hybridization between these and related species, so that "Christmas cacti" may now be found with white, pink, red, orange or purple flowers, and with blooming periods varying from Thanksgiving to late winter.

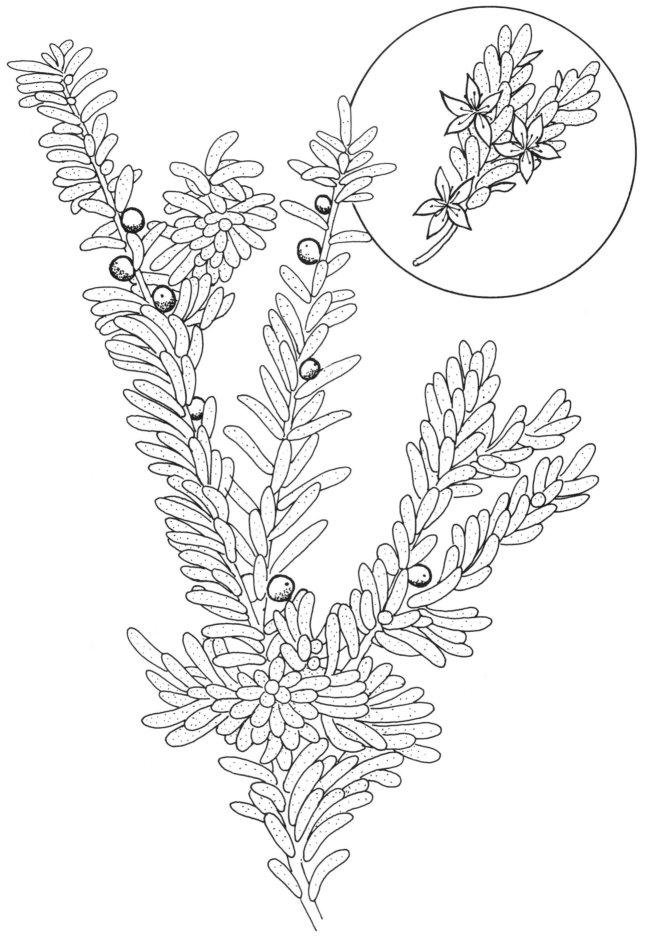

Opposite: **RHIPSALIS MESEMBRYANTHEMOIDES** (*Mistletoe cactus*). Brazil. Like all Rhipsalis species and their epiphytic relatives, it requires a loose, acidic, rich soil. Provide half shade and abundant water in summer. Reduce water in autumn, but once flowering has begun, water reguarly and keep slightly warm. A highly desirable house plant, it provides abundant flowers which are produced in winter. They are followed by white berries which give this cactus its common name.

Above: **RHIPSALIDOPSIS ROSEA.** Brazil. A small, epiphytic, shrubby cactus which, like plants of the genus Rhipsalis to which it is related, requires a well-drained soil rich in leaf mold and a partly shaded environment with ample summer water. Keep above freezing and provide good light and weekly watering in winter. Mature plants have two types of stems: young shoots are three- or four-sided, but later segments are predominantly flat. In spring it bears many purplish-pink flowers.

EPIPHYLLUM ACKERMANNII. A hybrid of two Mexican species. Despite its commonly used name, this plant is a hybrid between two epiphytic cacti, *Nopalxochia ackermannii* and *Heliocereus speciosus*. It has been in cultivation for many years and is still one of the most free-flowering of the Epiphyllum hybrids. It requires the usual cultural conditions for epiphytic cacti, and thrives in a soil rich in leaf mold. *E. ackermannii* produces its huge red flowers in spring. Other hybrid Epiphyllums can be obtained in a wide range of flower colors and combinations.

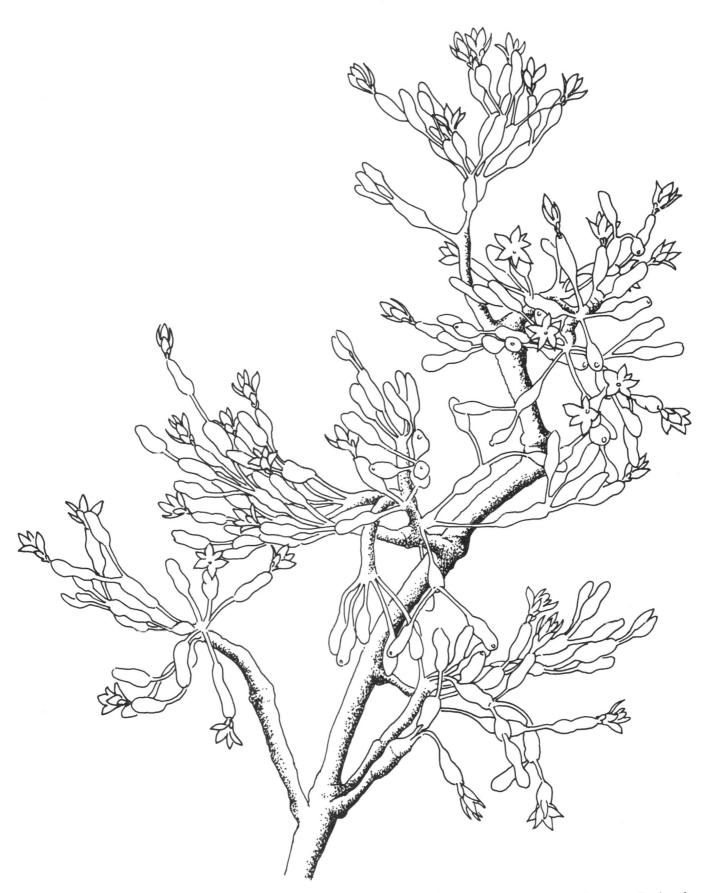

HATIORA SALICORNIOIDES (*Drunkard's dream*). Brazil. Hatiora grows as a hanging or erect branching epiphyte which may have branches several feet long. It makes an excellent hanging-basket plant, requiring half sun, a loose, acid soil and abundant summer water. Reduce watering in late September, giving weekly water all winter. During the winter flowering period, keep in bright light and at a temperature above 55° F. Small yellow-orange flowers are produced at the tip of each stem. The "bottle-shaped" stem segments give this plant its common name.

(continued from copyright page)

also be added, especially for those species with heavy spines or dense white hairs. When a more porous soil mix is required, add sand or perlite. Bone meal, superphosphate, or sterilized leafmold may be added where a richer soil is indicated. A half-inch top dressing of sand or fine gravel will keep wet soil away from the plant body and reduce the likelihood of its rotting.

Containers without drainage holes should not be used for cacti, but any other type of pot will be fine, provided that the soil drains rapidly. Never let cactus plants stand in muddy soil or water-filled saucers. Desert cacti must always be given as much natural sunlight as possible when in active growth, preferably unobstructed southern exposure.

Those cacti which are native to tropical jungles and woodlands usually grow as epiphytes, that is, plants anchored to the trunks or branches of other plants in partly shaded locations. Members of the *Zygocactus*, *Rhipsalis*, *Schlumbergera* and *Epiphyllum* groups, to name a few, will require warmer winter temperatures, more water, a looser, more acidic potting soil, and less sunlight than the desert or prairie types. Many will grow well in a fluorescent light garden. As a bonus, their flowering periods are often in winter, when other cacti are dormant.

The "Christmas cactus," *Zygocactus truncatus* and its hybrids, can be induced to flower by keeping it at 50° F. and rather dry for 6 to 8 weeks in October and November. Be careful that the plants get no more than 10 hours of natural or artificial light during that period. Other epiphytes may also need a rest period for best flowering.

Cacti may be propagated from seed or cuttings. It usually requires several years until seedlings reach blooming size. Branches or offsets may be cut off cleanly where they arise from the plant body and allowed to dry for at least a month before they are planted in damp, pure sand. Once roots have developed, the cuttings are transplanted to the usual soil mix.

For this book we have chosen cacti which are especially unusual or attractive. Common names have been given to only a small percentage of the thousands of cacti which are known to exist, and they should not be relied on for identification, since the same name is often applied to different species in different areas. We hope that as you enjoy coloring the cacti in this book, you will become more familiar with this fascinating plant family and be encouraged to grow them yourself.

Carolyn S. Ripps

INDEX OF SCIENTIFIC NAMES

Aporocactus flagelliformis, 39
Ariocarpus fissuratus, 18
Astrophytum asterias, 7
Astrophytum capricorne, 25
Austrocylindropuntia salmiana, 26
Aylostera deminuta, 38
Aztekium ritteri, 24

Carnegiea gigantea, 22
Cephalocereus senilis, 5
Coryphantha vivipara, 17

Dolicothele longimamma, 2

Echinocactus grusonii, 31
Echinocereus pentalophus, 27
Echinocereus triglochidiatus, 29
Echinofossulocactus multicostatus, 9
Encephalocarpus strobiliformis, 6
Ephiphyllum ackermannii, 44
Epithelantha micromeris, 15

Frailea pygmaea, 33

Gymnocalycium baldianum, 13
Gymnocalycium mihanovichii, 10
Gymnocalycium mihanovichii v. friedrichiae "Hibotan," 10
Gymnocalycium venturianum, 13

Hatiora salicorniodes, 45
Homalocephala texensis, 36

Leuchtenbergia principis, 30

Lobivia famatimensis, 34
Lophophora williamsii, 4

Mammillaria hahniana, 14
Mammillaria plumosa, 21
Mammillaria wildii, 12
Melocactus intortus, 37

Neobesseya missouriensis, 19
Notocactus haselbergii, 40
Notocactus rutilans, 23

Opuntia basilaris, 1
Opuntia bigelovii, 3
Opuntia salmiana, 26

Parodia sanguiniflora, 32
Pediocactus knowltonii, 35
Pelecyphora aselliformis, 11
Pereskia aculeata, 20

Rebutia deminuta, 38
Rhipsalidopsis rosea, 43
Rhipsalis mesembryanthemoides, 42

Schumbergera gaertneri, 41
Selenicereus grandiflorus, 28
Setiechinopsis mirabilis, 16
Stenocactus multicostatus, 9

Toumeya papyracantha, 8

Zygocatus truncatus, 41